My Brother has a Thing....

...and I want one!

A Sibling's view of Autism

...just for Ben

All Rights Reserved ©2018 Rachel Jackson

Authors note:

In early January I sat down and wrote The Thing – A Young Boy's journey with Asperger Syndrome for my 7 year old son who is diagnosed with High Functioning Asperger's.

It wasn't a plan of mine to become an author...

but it seemed to happen that way.

The Thing progressed rapidly from a scribbled set of words to a finished and beautifully illustrated product with the help of many friends, family and complete strangers and it started to be a subject of conversation in my house.

In June my youngest son returned from school with the first of 3 letters which he described as "naughty letters". I had never received any such note regarding my youngest – but many about my eldest.

"It was probably the Thing"

...he proudlly told me – I must have one too!

...and I suddenly realised that I had painted a picture that a Thing was the new cool accessory to have – and that mum wrote books about you if you had a Thing!

My youngest son is the missing character in The Thing.
The silent partner. The unsung hero.

This is <u>his</u> story.

My brother has a Thing
        ...and *I* want one.

My mum says *he* was born with it,
        and he's not the only one.

The Thing's called "a disorder"
        – or so the adults say.

I don't like *any* 'orders'
        if it means I can't just play.

"Be quiet" they say, "his ears might hurt
                  Be careful what you do".

"Just walk away if he gets too rough
                  or he might hurt you too".

He goes to a "special school"
                  in a taxi every day.

They say he couldn't learn to play
                  the games that we all play.

My brother sometimes shouts at me
                He sometimes calls me names.

I've tried to help him understand
                the rules to all my games.

He never seems to listen long
                and doesn't seem to care.

I wish he wouldn't steal my toys
                and throw them everywhere.

I'm told off when I 'wind him up'
             but I don't think I do.

I just like making lots of noise
             like other children do.

I don't see why I have to help him
             when he's mean to me.

He doesn't let me in his room
             when I just want to see.

I wish sometimes I had a Thing
 that people talked about.

I'd tell my mum "it was the Thing"
 when bad stuff was found out!

I'd blame it for all kinds of times
 when I got into trouble.

And I'd say "That Thing – it made me mad"
 when I just want a cuddle.

My brother has a Thing in him
        but I've not got one too.

Everybody talks about it
        – they don't know what to do.

I sometimes think they're scared of it
        the way they make a fuss.

To me, I think my brother's
        just like all the rest of us.

He gets a little crazy
          when he needs a run outside,

and he needs a hug like I do
          when I'm feeling bad inside.

He sometimes wants to jump about
          – he's moving all the time,

...but other times he's really quiet
          and he loves his cuddle time.

I know sometimes he's really sad
                and doesn't like The Thing.

He doesn't go to parties
                and he misses everything.

He finds it hard to stop himself
                and often makes mistakes.

It's like a train that's off the rails
                and can't put on its brakes.

My brother has a Thing...
            and that's mostly fine with me.

He's extra strong and really fast
            and great at climbing trees.

He tickles me and makes me laugh
            and sometimes when I'm sad

He holds my hand and takes me home
            or tells our mum and dad.

My brother has a Thing he does –
          ...and I have it too.

I share it with him every day and
          we work out what to do.

So next time when you meet us
          please...just remember this:

I love my brother very much..
          ....**exactly as he is!**

Parent / Carers Notes:

This book is designed to be read **s l o w l y** with your child and to be an interactive experience
– in whatever way it works with your child.

It only offers one perspective on how <u>one</u> sibling experiences his/her brother... your child's experience, may be different...and that's OK

Start a conversation with your child about what their brother does/says/has that makes them happy or sad? What do they worry about or think is unfair?

Their thoughts, language and descriptions may not make sense to you and may not be consistent
...but the conversation is what matters.

We are acknowledging that having a sibling with a diagnosis is not always easy – there are many parts of growing up that feel that way at times.

You may want to share your own feelings about your child's diagnosis that you sometimes struggle with. This connection is important. Be careful not to try to shift your child's thinking – it is OK just as it is.

When your child changes the subject...let it go.
It's time to move on and they may need time to process the story.

You may mention The Thing in passing later on and find that it has become something open to exploration
...or you may not. Either is fine.

Classroom ideas:

When presenting this story, try to read it out loud but stop to share the pictures with the children on each page – encouraging discussion of their own experiences.

It is important that every child's particular perspective be respected
— **we are all different**.

There is an opportunity for all children to relate to The Thing – or to the brother – as the boys in the story do.

This does not need to be a targeted discussion about Autism or ASD
— but about relationships and issues that we struggle with at times but are learning to manage.

- Ask the children to think about how it might feel to have a sibling who has special needs.

- Open up a discussion about what we might do to help others feeling this way…and explore how maybe the *way* in which we help might need to be different.

- Encourage all the children to draw a picture of what their Thing might look like; what it might do. Ask them how they feel about it.

About the Author:

Rachel studied Psychology at Royal Holloway University of London before training in counselling, coaching and NLP. She worked for 6 years in London as management consultant and went self employed in 2007 with a view to shifting her own work-life balance.

Whilst travelling independently around South East Asia she met her South African partner, Brad and they settled where Rachel grew up in rural Suffolk.

Rachel is now the mother of two boys – Leo (7½) and Ben (5¾). She balances her own coaching, facilitation and leadership development company – Changing Dialogues Ltd with the challenges of bringing up a family.

Leo was diagnosed in 2015 with High Functioning Asperger's. At risk of exclusion from successive local primary schools he has been welcomed for over two years in a fabulous Pupil Referral Unit near his home.
Now taking daily taxi-treks to attend school in Cambridge....the nearest facility equipped for academically able autistic children with behavioural issues, Leo is just beginning the next phase in his own journey with Asperger's.

Rachel dedicates this book with love to all the incredible friends, family, teachers, support workers and complete strangers who have helped both her and her family on this extraordinary journey.

Rachel...has her own thing!

Find out more about Rachel's 'day-job' at www.changingdialogues.com

About the Illustrator:

Zeke Clough is an illustrator based in Todmorden, best known...so far...for his distinctive sleeve artwork for electronic musicians such as Shackleton and Ekoplekz. His partner of eight years has 14 year old autistic twins who go to a specialist communication school.

Zeke's love of comic strips and drawing has proved to be an effective way to communicate with the boys. When they were younger their favourite toys were included in the comics - they either give advice or learned along with the boys. Many a meltdown or hazardous situation was circumvented by a quickly drawn explanatory comic strip!

Zeke also works for a mental health charity supporting school children to develop an understanding of the importance of good mental health and providing them with a language to discuss these issues. His illustrations also support his work with refugees/asylum seekers and adults with mental health difficulties.

In recent years, Zeke has been commissioned to support delegates at a number of neurodiversity conferences –drawing graphic notes to recall their learning effectively.
In the future he hopes to publish his social stories more widely, and to continue to explore mental health and autism related issues through comic strips and animation.

Zeke too has his things!

see more of Zeke's work at www.zekeclough.co.uk

The right of Rachel Jackson to be identified as the author of this work has been asserted by her in accordance with the Copyright acts.

Copyright © Rachel Jackson 2018
First published: September 2018

Available direct from the author at Changing Things Publishing
racheljackson@theaspergerthing.com

ISBN: 978 1999676 93 3

The Thing and the character created by Zeke Clough are registered as a Class 28 trademark UK000033308924

All rights reserved. No other part of this publication may be reproduced, stored in a retrieval system or transmitted in any form or by any means, electronic, mechanical, photocopying, recording or otherwise, without prior permission of the Publisher.

Find out more about The Thing and hear about new events and book releases at facebook.com/theaspergerthing

Zeke Clough....you too are the unsung hero in this series. Thank you so much for being my partner-in-crime.

www.ingramcontent.com/pod-product-compliance
Lightning Source LLC
Chambersburg PA
CBHW061806070526
44586CB00023B/2738